The Magical Means
of Poetry

Ananya Maskara

BookLeaf
Publishing

Presentation by *BookLeaf Publishing*

Web: www.bookleafpub.com

E-mail: info@bookleafpub.com

ISBN: 9789357618625

First edition 2023

I Am…

I am social and a reader
I wonder what the character will do next
I hear the books calling out to me to be read
I see the characters coming to life as I dive in
I want to stay in the fantasy forever
I am social and a reader

I pretend I am of the story as well
I feel the story touch my heart
I touch the sea, the dragon, and the crown
I worry the story won't have a happy ending
I cry as the character gets hurt and lost

I am social and a reader

I understand the character will heal
I say our friendship will be everlasting
I dream of the story throughout the night
I try to leave this dream untouched
I hope the characters will continue to live happy
I wish this story will come back to life for one
day more
As I dive into another book I leave the last one
in my heart
I am social and a reader

A World of Wonders

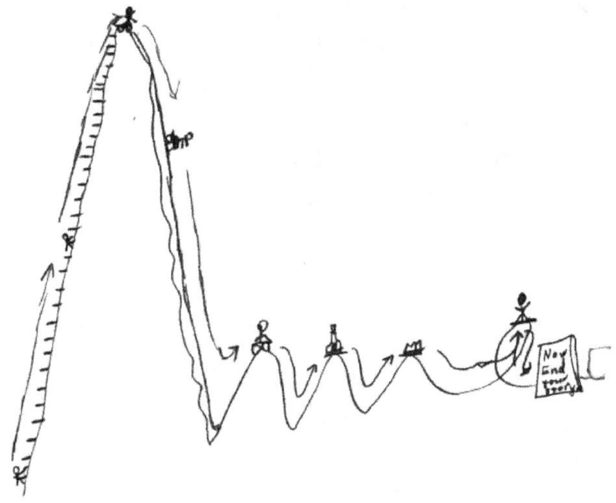

A world of wonders,
what a sight,
You can walk the tundras,
or have a fright.
You can share one's thoughts,
or sail a boat,
or ride a jaguar,
That's what I sought.
You can climb a cliff,
or swim the oceans,
become a king,

or start to sniff.
You can share one's tears,
or share one's laughter,
have some cheers,
or live happily ever after.
A world of wonders,
an amazing adventure.
Now end your story,
but keep it thereafter.

Over the Moon and into Space

Over the moon and into space,
there is a land,
a secret place.
There are holes,
that travel through time,
a nickel would work,
but the best is a dime.
Tons of mysteries lurk,
behind the stars so bright,
some bubbles are fast,

even faster than light.
Though the sound is none,
through this limitless land,
there is adventure a ton,
through these galaxies so grand.
From the top of my head,
to the tip of my toes,
let's follow this tune,
and see where it goes.
Over the moon and into space.

Silly Susan Soffee!!

Susan Soffee bought a toffee,
but she wished that it were red.
How she waited,
how she debated,
just because it was brown instead.

In the attic,
with some panic,
She stood alone without a light.
Her parents tell her "Do chores first",
and "learn to do them right".

Susan Soffee bought some coffee,
but she hated the cup that was red.
She looked at her watch,
and said "Oh my gosh!",
and threw the coffee away.
Then she strode outside the store,
and ran without delay.

My Mother's Care

To raise me with,
a pure heart as if gold,
you kept me in a tower,
blocking the cold.
A tower filled with,
so much love, and care,
that made me so tough,
and ever so fair.

When the cold blows away,
I breathe in the air,
remembering what you did,
when I was so frail,
Mumma,
Thank you for all that you do,
I could not have done anything,
without you.

Glaciers

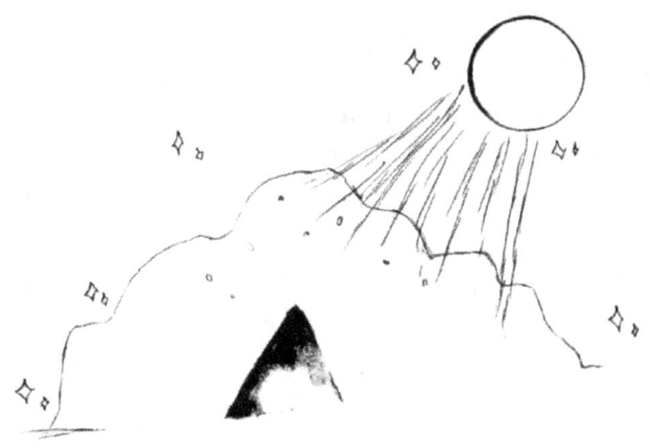

Glaciers, rivers that froze from cold,
pieces of memories,
that hold truth, strong and bold.

Mystic lands,
that shimmer and shine,
where concealed mysteries like to dine.
When the beams of moonlight,
initiate to glisten,
the mysteries cease,
and commence to listen,
to hear the sound,

of the twinkling lullabies.
Then the glacier lets the mysteries flow,
who then dance with a nightly glow.

Some dance the truth,
others the false,
a few sing some songs,
while the rest just have fun.
But all mysteries, stay a mystery,
while the glacier meets its destiny.

The Opposite Nightmare

Imagine you,
being you,
in a world completely new.

You look the same,
and dress the same,
but act in a way completely lame.

You used to read a book or two,
but now do nothing of that sort.
Instead of that,
you watch TV,
and hate to learn and hate to read.
You wish to end this terrible nightmare,
but first you must take an oath,
and swear,
to never be the one,
in your dream.
Once you are done,
you are free to leave,
but always remember,
that the oath,
will always be there to haunt your dreams.

Recycle Right!

People recycle, reuse, and reduce,
They use some old papers,
And make something new.
They use creativity,
Let their juices flow,
Their crafting ability,
And what do you know,
A beautiful thing-a-bob,
Lies in front of you.
Now that goal is gone,
There is more to do,
Recycle Right,
And make something new.
Sort the cans, papers, and plastic too,
It keeps you organized,
And resourceful-too true.
Always remember,
The two steps to do so,
Quickly register,
Before you do go,
Recycling Right!,
Is the new goal for you,
So always remember,
The two steps paired to two.

The Islands of Adventure

The Islands of Adventure,
where mystical mountains hide,
they can be full of archers,
or even unicorns,
that fly with pride.

The Mountains of Daring Ride,
which do not try to hide,
though still they do not,
boast with pride.
They are not slow,
still they are so kind,
they love to find and go,

on a wild and daring ride.

If this is you,
and please do be true,
then you do belong,
in the Islands of Prong,
and so on,
and so on.

Potion of Love

Phoenix tears of healing,
makes the potion that most desire.
The Phoenix fears of feeling,
Anger, which wires most hearts' desires.
The Phoenix feels the Truth of Love,
which makes most people go haywire,
The Phoenix heals the Truth of Love,
that She and only a Dove can hire.
The Truth of Love,
pairs with the Phoenix and the Dove,
Who then await everlasting harmony,
in the magical world of Witchcraft and
Wizardry.

A Secret Library

A secret library,
full of books.
Where people listen,
to beautiful hooks.
Hooks that pull them in,
without a glance,
and keep them there,
till the joyous dance.

A secret library,
full of treasures.

The beautiful Fairy,
stays for good measures.

With the books,
surrounding each corner,
know which one took,
the foreigner's order.
Be the detective,
in the books,
and don't decide,
on just the looks.
Don't get tricked,
by the hooks,
and you'll do good,
on the examiner's quotes.
Now solve the mystery,
rewrite history,
and end your story,
in the secret library.
A secret library,
is an adventurer's,
most, best, friend.

Halloween Terror! (Say in a spooky tone)

Pumpkins,
Rumpkins,
and Magic Monsters.
All are very similar,
creepy haunters.
Halloween terror,
nightmares forever,
plus ghosts and goblins,
What a fright!
October 31st,
is Halloween night!

Muah ha ha ha ha ha!
say the Vampires,
the terror does scare everyone,
even the whole Empire.
Children trick-or-treating,
throughout the streets.
And people giving candy,
and plenty of other sweets.
Halloween is scary,
especially during the night.
So without of the candy,
Halloween's not right.
So, climb each and every step,
and then sit tight.
And then wait for the spookling,
magic to ignite.
Just have some fun,
on this night,
and you will have a blast,
if you do it right,
on Halloween night!
Muah ha ha ha ha!

A Musical Friend

The rhythm of music,
has its own beat.
And you do not know,
which kinds you will meet.
You make some music,
with maybe strings or keys.
Or maybe some woodblocks,
or glockenspiels.
The music's rhythm,
is like your friend.
It makes you feel different,
and mostly at the end.
Its feelings,
change your mood,

whether happy or sad.
Reminds you of food,
or all that you had.
Its melody warms your heart,
when you are stiff or alone.
It makes you feel tart,
when you are in your own zone.
So listen to music,
It keeps the cold away.
And remember the rhythm,
to keep the warmth your way.

Two Playful Kittens

There are two little kittens,
that are playing with yarn.
They like wearing mittens,
and stay in the barn.
Those two little kittens,
love to play all day.
They hung out their mittens,
in their sincere way.

Their cuteness alarm,
has no limit.
And their friendly farm,
has no hatred in it.
They race through the fields,

playing in the crops.
For the Farmer they yield,
and then tip their tops.
So whenever you see,
these cute little kittens,
there is nothing they wish more,
than a pair of two little mittens.

The Beach's Potion

The sun sets on the horizon,
when evening strikes on the beach.
I hold my shovel made of iron,
and swim to the bucket that's out of my reach.
And then the while as I grab it,
I hold it close to me.
And witness what it is like,
walking out of the sea.
While climbing stair by stair,
I roll a towel around me.
A shiver straightens my hair,
when the sky really does astound me.

Wonderful as it is,
here by the sandy seas.
The sand-castle making,
and the swaying palm trees.
So on the ride home,
while I missed the ocean.
I thought of what it did to me,
almost like a potion.
What it did to that mad little me,
maybe it was washed away?
It turned me into a humble little bee,
and I felt nothing but swaying.
Then for the first time in my life,
I thanked the Beach.
And listened and remembered,
on what it had to teach.
Staying calm,
is the way to win your battle.
So do not panic,
because you're not riding cattle.

A Special Selection of Minerals

A rock collection,
with shimmering stones.
Stays in a section,
that glistens and glows.
Solar beams hit,
from the window they meet,
makes them look lit,
though they have no feet.
When imagined they would've,
they would duel with a race.
Run if they could've,
to beat the opponent they face.
So the next time you learn a spell,
to make an object come alive,

maybe revive a rock or two,
and see if they survive.

The Unknown

Deep beneath the seas,
of utter mystery.
There lies some peace,
not mentioned in history.
Those beautiful caves,
that live miles below,
don't sway in the waves,
tons of studies show.
Though no studies prove,
"Aliens don't exist",
Many unexplored caverns,
lie beneath the mist.
No one dares,

to dive right in,
'Cause no one knows,
what lies within.

The Best of Friends

We're the best of friends,
me and you.
We love playing,
through and through.
We love
dancing, books, and music too.

The forever of friends,
you and me.
We love to jump and climb the trees.
We go together,
like honey and bees.

I know our friendship,
will last forever,
even if we are not together.
We are friends forever.

9 789357 618625